The Wild World of Animals

Wolves

Life in the Pack

by Lola M. Schaefer

Consultant:
Dwight Lawson, Ph.D.
General Curator
Zoo Atlanta

Bridgestone Books
an imprint of Capstone Press
Mankato, Minnesota

Bridgestone Books are published by Capstone Press
151 Good Counsel Drive, P.O. Box 669, Mankato, Minnesota 56002
http://www.capstone-press.com

Library of Congress Cataloging-in-Publication Data
Schaefer, Lola M., 1950–
    Wolves: life in the pack/by Lola M. Schaefer.
    p. cm.—(The wild world of animals)
    Includes bibliographical references and index.
    ISBN 0-7368-0830-2
1. Wolves—Juvenile literature. [1. Wolves.] I. Title. II. Series.
QL737.C22 S34 2001
599.773—dc21   00-010185

Summary: An introduction to wolves describing their physical characteristics, habitat, young, food, enemies, and relationship to people.

Editorial Credits
Erika Mikkelson, editor; Karen Risch, product planning editor; Linda Clavel, designer and illustrator; Kimberly Danger and Heidi Schoof, photo researchers

Photo Credits
Craig Brandt, 4, 8
Daybreak Imagery/Robert McKemie, cover
GeoIMAGERY/Robert Winslow, 6, 10, 20
PhotoDisc, Inc., 1
Photri Inc./Tom Walker, 12
Visuals Unlimited, 16; Tom Walker, 14; Rob Kieft, 18

1 2 3 4 5 6 06 05 04 03 02 01

Table of Contents

ears

eyes

jaw

legs

tail

Wild Wolves

All wolves belong to the wild dog family. Wolves have long, strong legs. They have long jaws filled with pointed teeth. Thick fur covers wolves' bodies. Wolves also have long tails.

Wolves Are Mammals

Wolves are mammals. Mammals are warm-blooded animals that have a backbone. Female mammals feed milk to their young. Most mammals are covered with hair. A wolf's thick coat protects it from rain, snow, and cold.

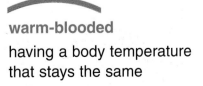

warm-blooded
having a body temperature that stays the same

FUN FACTS Wolves mark their territory. They leave their scent on the trees, bushes, and grass around their territory. A wolf can tell if a scent belongs to a wolf in its pack or to a wolf from another pack.

A Wolf's Habitat

Wolves live in many habitats. They make their homes in forests, mountains, or deserts. Their bodies adapt to different climates. Wolves need food and water near their habitats. Most wolves give birth in dens that are caves or hollow tree trunks.

habitat
the place where an animal lives

Life in the Pack

Many wolves travel and hunt in a group called a pack. The wolves in a pack are friendly and loyal to one another. One male wolf and one female wolf lead each pack. Most wolf packs have five to eight members.

loyal
to be faithful to someone or something

FUN FACTS

A wolf's sense of smell is one hundred times greater than a human's sense of smell. A wolf can pick up the scent of prey 3 to 4 miles (5 to 6 kilometers) away.

Fearless Hunters

Wolves hunt live prey. Wolves use their strong senses to hunt. They can hear and smell deer, elk, rabbits, and other prey from miles away. Wolves use their sharp teeth to kill the prey. The wolf pack shares the fresh meat.

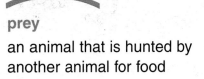

prey
an animal that is hunted by another animal for food

Mating and Birth

Male and female wolves mate in early spring. In a wolf pack, only the male and female leaders usually mate. The female wolf gives birth to a litter of pups about 60 days later. Most litters have four to six young wolves. They are born in dens.

mate

to join together to produce young

Wolf Pups

Young wolves are called pups. Pups cannot see or hear at first. Pups are strong enough to leave the den after one month. Older wolves in the pack bring food to the pups. Pups begin to travel and hunt with the pack when they are one year old.

Enemies

People are the wolf's greatest enemy. In the past, people killed wolves for their fur. Wolves sometimes attack livestock. People hunt, trap, and kill wolves that come near their homes or farms. People build roads and clear forests. This takes away some of the wolves' habitat.

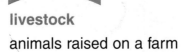

livestock
animals raised on a farm

The red wolf is an endangered animal. Many people are working to increase the number of red wolves living in the wild.

Wolves and People

For many years, all wolves were endangered animals. People worked to increase the number of wild wolves. Wolves play an important part in nature. They kill weak or sick animals that cannot survive in the wild. People have passed laws to protect wolves.

endangered

in danger of having all of one kind of animal die out

Hands On: Wolf Tag

Wolves work together in packs to hunt for food. Wolves chase and surround their prey. Each wolf takes a turn biting the animal. The wolves kill the animal in this way. You can learn how teamwork helps wolves find the food they need to survive.

What You Need

Several friends
A large open area

What To Do

1. Choose one person to be a wolf. The rest of the people are deer.
2. The wolf should try to tag as many deer as he or she can. The deer can run around to try to escape the wolf. Tagged deer should sit down on the ground.
3. Did it take a long time for the wolf to tag all the deer?
4. Now, try teamwork to tag the deer. Have two or three people be a wolf pack. The rest of the people are deer.
5. The wolves should surround each deer and tag the person out. Deer should sit on the ground after they are tagged.
6. Did it take less time when the wolves worked together?

Wolves find food more easily when they work together in a pack.

Words to Know

adapt (uh-DAPT)—to change to fit into a new environment

climate (KLYE-mit)—the usual weather in a place

den (DEN)—the place where a wild animal lives; wolf pups are born in dens.

litter (LIT-ur)—a group of animals born at the same time to the same mother

pack (PAK)—a group of animals that live and travel together; wolves travel together in a pack.

prey (PRAY)—an animal that is hunted by another animal for food

scent (SENT)—the odor or smell of something

Read More

León, Vicki. *A Pack of Wolves.* Close-Up. New York: New Discovery Books, 1999.

Markle, Sandra. *Growing Up Wild: Wolves.* New York: Atheneum Books for Young Readers, 2001.

Otto, Carolyn B. *Wolves.* Scholastic Science Readers. New York: Scholastic, 2000.

Internet Sites

The BoomerWolf Web Site
http://www.boomerwolf.com
International Wolf Center
http://www.wolf.org
NOVA Online: Wild Wolves
http://www.pbs.org/wgbh/nova/wolves/

Index